- Successful Dating -

No More Frogs
Pisces

19 February – 20 March

by
Cathrine Dahl

CONTENTS

- Successful Dating -
No More Frogs

by Cathrine Dahl

No More Frogs - Successful Dating is your one-stop dating guide. No unnecessary blah-blah. The information is right here, at your fingertips.

This guide can be used in several ways. It's a handy tool when you want to prepare yourself a little. It can give you an advantage when going on a date or getting to know someone you've just met - or even someone you've known for a while.

Although this guide can help you angle your approach, remember to be true to yourself. Have fun, be wise, follow your heart - and keep your feet on the ground!

- Cathrine Dahl

Preface:
A few words about compatibility, and why compatibility guides can give you the wrong idea.

So you've met this Gemini you really, really like, but you're a Scorpio, and the compatibility guides say you're a lousy match. Guess what? That's rubbish!

Some compatibility guides offer a very simplistic approach, claiming that your best matches are the star signs within the same element as you:

Fire: Aries, Leo and Sagittarius
Earth: Taurus, Virgo and Capricorn
Air: Gemini, Libra and Aquarius
Water: Cancer, Scorpio and Pisces

Other guides are slightly more specific, declaring that we are compatible with star signs within our astrological polarity.

Yin: Taurus, Virgo, Capricorn, Cancer, Scorpio and Pisces
Yang: Aries, Leo, Sagittarius, Gemini, Libra and Aquarius

Doesn't look too good, does it? The most optimistic approach has removed half of the population from your dating pool. It doesn't make any sense. The true picture is far more promising...

One star sign, two very different personalities

Each of us has a unique astrological thumbprint determined by the sun, the moon and the planets. The most important factors being your ascending star (ascendant), the sun (star sign) and the moon (feelings).

Let's make it simple

Imagine your star sign being a melody. All the other aspects (the unique positioning of the moon and the planets) are sound effects, applied by a producer with a mixer.

The combination of rhythm, depth and base creates your unique sound. Another person with the same star sign will get his own sound mix and end up with a different beat.

Your personal melody can create wonderful harmonies with star signs you're not supposed to get on with – and nothing but noise with signs that are meant to be matches. You won't find out until you get to know each other.

Let's get to know your date...

THE MALE

YOUR DATE: PISCES
19 February–20 March

The Essence of him

Dreamy – romantic – absent-minded; loses track of time – sensitive – creative – inquisitive – happy (seemingly) – naïvely charming – genuine – good-intentioned – spontaneous – intense and confident in bed – kind – adventurous – loves beauty – empathetic – knowledgeable – perceptive – has a good memory – unpretentious – conflict-avoidant

...and remember: He may come across as a Man – and sometimes even a toughie – but at heart, he's a big kid. It's his boyish side that draws him to strong, cheerful, smart and playful women.

Blind Date – speedy essentials

Who's waiting for you?

See the way he looks at you when you enter the room? His easy smile may give the impression that he's not taking the date seriously and that he's just doing it for kicks. Not the case! This guy's got a unique way of sparking your interest, but you won't notice this until you're hooked. He's genuinely charming, and there's nothing fake about him. Forget about the guys who've been trying to impress you with big cars, fat wallets and inflated egos. This guy really wants to get to know you – and he'll have a great time doing it.

Emergency fixes for embarrassing pauses

Don't worry, the chances of an embarrassing pause with the Pisces man are slim to none. He'll either be absorbed in whatever you're telling him or busy sharing his knowledge with you – and this guy knows a little about a lot. The only women who can manage to shut him up and send his eyes darting around the room are ones who are shallow, negative or nagging.

Your place or mine?

Sex on a first date is not typical of Mr Pisces. But if he really likes you, and both mood and situation turn passionate, he won't say no. He's got a romantic streak, so he won't suggest a quick one in the backseat of his car. But don't be fooled into thinking he's a softie. He'll drop his boyish nature along with his clothes and display himself as a true Man!

Checklist, before you dash out to meet him:

Clear your agenda – at least from early meetings

(hint: It might get late...)

Make a fun comment when you see him

(hint: It'll set the tone and fascinate him)

Tone down tattoos and piercings

(hint: Classic femininity will do)

Save some unique music or images on your phone

(hint: Inspire him)

Have a good appetite

(hint: No dieting. Enjoy your food – and life)

Tip: Avoid discussing gossip and negative news. He is attracted to positive and humorous women with sparkling personalities. But don't shine so bright that you command all of the attention.

CHAPTER 1

PREPARE YOURSELF

Catch his eye, capture his attention
Top 10 attention grabbers

1. Be assertive and take the initiative – without being bossy.
2. In conversation, approach a topic or everyday event from a new angle.
3. Be positive! Make sure your glass is half-full – or even better, just full.
4. Bring out the smile in your eyes and laughter in your voice.
5. Ask him out-of-the-ordinary questions.
6. Be playful. A childlike attitude will help him relax.
7. Be sparkling and fun.
8. Show your feelings, but don't get emotional.
9. Listen without prejudice.
10. Show off your feminine side and avoid anything aggressive.

The SHE. The woman!

The Pisces man seeks fun in his life. He wants to explore the world, and he treats every little thing as an adventure. But he also needs to feel safe and loved – and like a man. This means that his woman must be a little bit of everything: a fun companion, a sensitive, romantic and tender partner, a safe haven when life kicks his butt, and a hot lover. Seem unrealistic? Don't worry. Mr Pisces has the ability to bring out different sides of women, and it happens naturally.

The Essence of her
Feminine – romantic – sensitive – has a great sense of humour – strong– open-minded – has a upbeat voice – has smiling eyes – smart – alert – informed and willing to expand her mind – loves and explores life – introduces him to interesting experiences and people – attentive to his needs – takes the initiative – inspires him to explore life

Pisces arousal meter
From 0 to 100... In an hour or less, as long as the setting is right and he gets the encouragement he needs.

Remember: Be true to yourself

It doesn't matter if he is the most stunning guy you've ever met – if you don't match, you don't match. You may be able to put on a show for a while to hold his attention, but what's the point? We can't please everybody. We all have different needs, dreams, tastes and preferences. There's no such thing as a one-size-fits-all lover. Be yourself, and be true to who you are – always!

Very important: Never make him feel cornered. If you squeeze him too hard, he'll fly out of your hands like a bar of wet soap.

CHAPTER 2

THE FIRST DATE

Getting your foot in the door
The basics

Positive, laid back attitude! Greet him with a smile – a genuine one, not an 'I'm hot' smile. Be laid back about the date, as if you were going out with a friend.

Expose your mind. Make sure to have some interesting facts or topics up your sleeve – something that will make him pay attention. Surprise him with knowledge that is a little out of the ordinary.

Fun suggestions. There's no need to leave all the decisions about the date to him. Suggest something new and different.

Be cool, be playful. Drop him a few subtle hints, but don't be too obvious about your intentions – even if you're really into him.

Masculinity rocks. Although he likes strong women, he gets a kick out of someone who makes him feel like a Man. Show him that you truly enjoy being around him.

Listen with an open mind. Respect his opinions, even when you disagree. It doesn't hurt to be humorous about it.

Whatever you do...

• **DON'T** defend your principles for the sake of it.

• **DON'T** give the impression that you know best.

• **DON'T** be critical or negative.

• **DON'T** sport tattoos or piercings.

• **DON'T** wear outfits that are overly suggestive.

Remember,
If you feel the need to approach sensitive topics, make sure to be diplomatic

- **DON'T** keep looking at your watch or say you're worried

about getting to bed too late.

- **DON'T** tell him to calm down or get a grip on reality.

- **DON'T** question his masculinity.

- **DON'T** be insensitive.

- **DON'T** flirt with other men.

about it! If he feels provoked and hurt, and he may turn his back on you.

Signs you're in - or not

Even if you've spent a nice, long evening together, it doesn't necessarily mean you're in – at least not romantically. He may find you interesting, fun and great company, but triggering his passion is something else entirely. This is what can make this guy such a challenge to figure out. Behaviours that would indicate serious interest from other men do not mean the same coming from him. His enthusiasm may simply signal that he thinks you're cool. However, there are some sure ways to know that you've hit a home run:

Chances are he will...

- make it clear that he'd like to see you again
- include you in future plans of things he'd like to do or try out
- prefer to talk to you even when he's surrounded by people
- seem genuinely interested in your views
- act enthusiastic when he's around you
- text to let you know you're on his mind

Not your type? Making an exit

Making an exit is easy, provided he doesn't have deep feelings for you – and this would be really odd. In his world, passion feeds on mutual interest; his flame cannot burn by itself. In any case, the quicker you make an exit, the better. Hanging around and pretending to be interested when you're not, hoping to spare his feelings, will make things a lot worse. The best approach is to be rational and polite about it. Let him know that you really enjoyed his company, but imply that you both might find greater happiness elsewhere.

If he has fallen deeply for you, you may need to divert his attention to your less attractive sides (feel free to produce a few fake ones). By making him see you in a different light, you'll show Mr Pisces that he was wrong about you all along – then he'll kick himself for being so stupid and take off.

Foolproof exit measures:

Sure, these are brutal – but they'll work. Be prepared to look like a bit of a jerk!

- Ridicule his sensitivity and question his masculinity
- Be rigid in your views, and toss in a few derogatory and discriminating remarks for good measure
- Forget to call or text him back
- Express your admiration for successful and ambitious men
- Tell him that men ought to focus more on exercising their biceps than their brains
- Respond to his suggestions with a yawn and a negative comment

CHAPTER 3

SEX'N STUFF

Seductive moves:
How to get him in the mood:

If he really likes you, getting him warmed up shouldn't be difficult at all. The fun thing about this guy is that he's up for sex at the weirdest times, in the weirdest places. He's not necessarily a kinky dude, but if the situation arises ... well, why miss out on a good experience?

Preferences and erotic nature

The Pisces man gets a kick out of being slowly undressed – preferably by a slightly dominant woman (even though she's just pretending). Don't rush it. This guy enjoys a good foreplay. It may start in an office chair, in the kitchen while making dinner, taking a shower after working out, or while getting ready to go out... Show a little initiative, and be gentle and firm. Dancing can lead to passionate activities – no matter where you are. Even playing footsies can be a fun place to start. The gentle brushing of bodies against each other can get him in the mood very quickly. If you've invited him over for a hot date, make sure to light some candles. Remember, this guy is attracted to sensual women, so be tender, seductive and a little sassy.

Hitting the right buttons

Although every sign has areas that are more sensitive than others, individual sensitivity may vary quite a bit. Don't go body-blind. Honing in on these erogenous zones and forgetting the rest of him is not a good idea. Use his erogenous zones to create sparks while turning him on, and as a passion booster when it gets heated. Watch his body language – including the most obvious of signs! Open your mind to the sensuality of touch and taste.

Key areas
Feet and ankles

Get it on
With a Pisces man, a casual foot massage can turn into something far spicier. Ankles, toes and soles of feet are particularly sensitive for men born under this sign. You'll have loads of opportunities to arouse him this way.

Arouse him
Kick off your shoe while having dinner and touch his ankles gently under the table. At home, complete the foot massage with gentle kisses around his ankles; brush your lips over his toes and the soles of his feet. Apply a little pressure to avoid tickling him. Even when you work your way up to sex, don't neglect his feet. Try positions that allow you to fondle and touch his feet. Let him explore you with his toes. You may be in for a pleasant surprise...

Surprise him

This man is a dreamer, and this carries over into his erotic life. Ask him about his fantasies and – as long as they're not too far out there – whether he would like to do more than just fantasise...

Spice it up

Rub his feet with warm oil. Let your hands slide around and between his toes, and round it off with gentle kisses.

Remember: This man is perceptive and picks up on hints easily. Be aware of how you come across, and don't send him mixed signals – he will notice all of them, and it will only confuse him.

His expectations

Be present! This man is no self-starter. It takes two to tango, especially when it comes to sex. If you seem reluctant or even a little ignorant, then you'll find he can't be bothered. There's no space in his bed for lazy partners.

Express pleasure. Besides wanting you to be active during sex, he also expects some sort of feedback. No, you don't have to be vocal about it. He's a good nonverbal communicator, too.

New ideas. Being assertive is a plus. Go ahead and expand his erotic horizons – he'll appreciate it. Remember, although he enjoys trying new things, anything too vulgar is a complete turn-off.

Bring it on! If you're passionate, liberated, impulsive and romantic, Mr Pisces will respond by transforming his boyish charm into hot, erotic masculinity.

Make it fun. A partner who can introduce him to new experiences will always make him happy.

Embrace his enthusiasm. Don't give him the 'look' if he suggests trying something unusual or having sex at the spur of the moment. This will hurt his feelings and probably turn him off you for quite some time.

Your sensual preferences
Quiz yourself and find out whether this man is for you.

Where on the scale are you?
1 = Don't agree | 3 = Sure | 5 = Agree!

1. Sensitivity is important to get maximum pleasure from sex.
One a scale for 1 to 5, you are : 1 - 2 - 3- 4 - 5

2. Sensuality ought to be experienced in the mind as well as the body.
One a scale for 1 to 5, you are : 1 - 2 - 3- 4 - 5

3. Playful impulsiveness can make sex feel more liberating and satisfying.
One a scale for 1 to 5, you are : 1 - 2 - 3- 4 - 5

4. Foreplay is the key to a wonderful sex life.
One a scale for 1 to 5, you are : 1 - 2 - 3- 4 - 5

Score 15–20: You may find yourself having sex often, simply because you manage to create the opportunities for it.
Score 10–14: You probably manage to communicate with your partner on many levels, which enables you to experience sex more deeply.
Score 5–9: Although there will be passion and fun between you, you may get a little confused about your partner's sensitivity. Don't think too much. Allow yourself to get carried away.
Score 1–4: His style may be a little sensitive, but he is open to suggestions. Communicate and guide him gently, and he may pump up the passion.

CHAPTER 4

GENERAL STUFF

The big picture

Keep in mind that the characteristics of a Pisces may vary quite a bit depending on where within the sign he was born, as well as a wide range of additional astrological factors. But for now, let's stick to the basics. Just remember: don't jump to conclusions as soon as you meet him. Give him room to shine. Get to know the man behind the sign.

His personality: Pros and cons

Pros
- Able to admit he was wrong
- Both masculine and sensitive
- Has an incredible memory
- Knowledgeable
- Empathetic
- Perceptive and understanding
- Positive and playful
- A romantic dreamer
- Easygoing
- Supportive and motivational
- Makes friends easily
- Seeks adventure
- Appreciates the beauty in life
- Enjoys style and quality

Cons
- Can get absorbed in himself
- Avoids difficult decisions
- Remembers negative things
- Absorbed his own interests
- Blunt and hurtful when upset
- Lives in his own world
- Avoids confrontation
- Argumentative when provoked
- Not particularly ambitious
- Indecisive; fails to commit
- Emotionally insecure
- Oversensitive
- Moody
- Overindulgent when stressed

Tip: How to show romantic interest

Appeal to his feelings. Pick up a book that means something to him, a bottle of wine you know he likes, or a little delicacy that tugs at his heartstrings. Anything personal will strike a chord with this man.

Romantic Vibes

Mr Pisces:
The romantic and adventurous partner

The essence

Hooked. As soon as he finds the woman, he won't let her go easily. Sweet messages, creative invitations, little gifts and an almost naïve openness are strong indications that Mr Pisces is hooked.

Romantic spotlight. When in love, he gives the woman centre stage in his life. Work, hobbies and friends are pushed down on his list of priorities – especially when the romance is new.

Going for it! He can be surprisingly assertive when he's made up his mind. Should you be so lucky to experience a Pisces in love, you'll find it very hard to say no.

Worth waiting for. Although he may wish you'd proclaim your love for him right away, he does realise that patience can be good, and sometimes even necessary. He will never pressure you, but he will give you subtle hints.

A true romantic. He will bring romance to your life from dawn to dusk – and even during the night, if you're awake.

Spoiling you. He'll call or text during the day to let you know he's thinking about you. He'll surprise you with breakfast in bed or buy a little something that he knows will mean a lot to you. In other words, he'll make life wonderful.

Tip: How to show erotic interest

Be playful about it – and direct, but not crude. Make your assertiveness feminine and flirty, and things will go to another level – provided you are in a setting that allows for it!

Erotic Vibrations

Mr Pisces:
The sensitive and playful lover

The essence

Surprise! The first time you encounter Mr Pisces in bed, you will probably be surprised. What happened to the sweet and gentle guy? Here, he'll transform into a passionate man who will take your breath away. Any trace of his shyness and insecurity will disappear.

No fiddling. Assertive, intense and hot ... this guy is a sensual dream who knows his way around women. There will be no nervous fiddling when he's around. This guy is no roaring Leo or fierce Scorpio. He's focused on the sensual sides to sex.

Expand your erotic mind. In his opinion, sex shouldn't be confined to the body; it should be a journey of the mind as well.

Dreams and fantasies. Some Pisces get a kick out of exploring erotic dreams and fantasies, but for most part, this man will prefer to have sex in nice, comfortable surroundings.

Impulsive. Sex is more than a once-a-week-on-a-Friday kind of thing for him. He is impulsive and may suggest sex at odd times (a sassy lunch break, etc.).

Just for kicks. Even though he is sexually assertive, he doesn't mind a dominant partner. Things can get steamy if a fully dressed woman asks him to take his clothes off!

CHAPTER 5

COMPATIBILITY QUIZ

Are you banging your head against the wall, or does he unleash your positive potential? Do you provoke him or bring out the best in him? Does he make you throw your arms up in exasperation, or do you feel inspired and complete in his company? Are the two of you headed towards doom or dream? Take the test to find out.

Question 1.
Are you able to see things from different perspectives?

A. Yes – it's important to avoid misunderstandings.
B. Mostly, provided I'm not angry or provoked.
C. Blah, blah, blah. I'm no shrink!

Question 2.
What do you do when your guy tells you about his dreams and everything he wants to achieve?

A. Listen, of course. However, I do take some of his ideas with a pinch of salt.
B. Yawn. My guy tends to live in his head. I prefer to focus on the real world.
C. I love a man with ideas. It inspires me and makes me more creative.

(cont.)

Question 3.
You're having a discussion, and it gets a little heated. What's your approach?

A. I always speak my mind, no matter what. If he can't take the heat, he should step away from the fire.
B. I try not to step on people's toes, but I tend to get passionate about topics that are important to me.
C. I feel we achieve more by listening and learning from each other. I'd try to keep the discussion from turning into an argument.

Question 4.
Do you participate actively when having sex?

A. Yes, of course. Sex is not just about receiving; it's about giving – and that can be a great turn-on in itself.
B. I'm not very assertive, and I prefer my partner to take the initiative.
C. It depends on my mood, really. Sometimes it's nice to be pampered; other times, I'm all over my partner.

Question 5.
How about erotic fantasies? Should they be kept secret, or...

A. The definition of a fantasy is something private and personal – and that's how they should stay!
B. Sharing fantasies with a man I trust can spice things up quite a bit...
C. I wouldn't mind talking about his fantasies, provided they're not too kinky. I may even share some of mine.

Question 6.
What kind of guy turns you on?

A. A romantic, caring type.
B. Someone who's sensual, intelligent and creative.
C. A masculine stud.

Question 7.
Do you believe there are guys who have genuine faith in the goodness of people?

A. I think so ... if not, the world would be a very cynical place.
B. The goodness of people? Sounds like something from the sixties. I want a real man – not a 'Peace, man!'
C. I think most people have an inherent sense of goodness – some guys more than others – and I like that.

Question 8.
You've been seeing this guy for a few weeks, and things are getting serious. How do you expect him to move the relationships forward?

A. Give me loads of freedom and leave it up to me to call him.
B. Spend as much time with me as possible.
C. Take the initiative, introduce me to his friends and suggest interesting things to do.

Question 9.
Do you find it easy to show your feelings?

A. I don't wear my heart on my sleeve, no. Why be vulnerable when I don't have to?
B. Sure. It's always good to talk about things – including feelings. It's the perfect way to establish trust.
C. I'm very sensitive, so emotions play a big part in my life.

Question 10.
You just met a guy, and the two of you hit it off. Would you prefer him to take it slow and ease into things, or are you eager to get to know him?

A. I definitely want to get to know him – fast!
B. Depends on the guy, really. If the chemistry is there, I don't mind things progressing naturally.
C. I'd prefer him to pull back a little. I never rush into things, even though it might be tempting at times.

SCORE	A	B	C
Question 1	10	5	1
Question 2	5	1	10
Question 3	1	10	5
Question 4	10	1	5
Question 5	1	10	5
Question 6	5	10	1
Question 7	5	1	10
Question 8	1	10	5
Question 9	1	5	10
Question 10	10	5	1

75 – 100

Once in a while, it just happens. The chemistry is there, love and romance grow quickly out of nowhere, and whatever seemed grey and boring in your life suddenly bursts with colour. This guy is like a magic wand ... and he probably has one, too. Should you ever have a moment of doubt about the relationship, call him. As soon as you hear his voice, your insecurities will disappear. You may not agree on everything, but this can actually be a good thing. It will allow you to explore each other's minds and widen your horizons. Enjoy!

51 – 74

If you let go, the two of you could get really into each other – and that's a pretty good start. So what if he doesn't aspire to become the next Mr Universe or spend hours at the gym, pumping his muscles? This is a good-looking guy with a relaxed attitude and a unique sensitivity. Sure, you may wish he could be more assertive at times. However, his energy, tenderness and consideration for others make up for his lack of high-flying ambition. This leaves a lot up to you. Why not make an effort to come up with some ideas and suggestions? Add a bit of adventure to a grey day. Not only will the two of you have fun together, but Mr Pisces will be even more hooked on you.

26 – 50

Have you started talking to yourself yet? Do you mumble under your breath when he loses track of time or forgets dates, shopping lists and appointments? Try to ignore the little hiccups. This man has got a 1000 things going on in his mind. Can you blame him for being absent-minded? Remember, he's a kid at heart. Nagging and criticising will yield nothing but bad vibes. He may even retreat into himself – and stay there until you can't take it anymore. There is one word you must remember: D-I-P-L-O-M-A-C-Y. If you fail on this, he'll fly out of your grip like a bar of soap that's been squeezed too hard. If you're looking for a super-masculine alpha male, you can forget Mr Pisces – he finds those guys pathetic, anyway. Don't try to turn him in to a muscular hunk, because you won't succeed. You'll have to either let him go or love him for who he is.

10 – 25

He may have been fun company at first, but how do you feel now? Is he holding you back? Does he lack the fierce energy you need to thrive? Are you becoming a little too independent for his sensitive nature? Do you crave a more ambitious guy who can get going without you kicking his butt? Love is wonderful; love is heavenly – but love requires a lot of work. Sometimes it's worth it and sometimes it's not You have to figure out whether this is love or temporary excitement – and if it's worth it, or if you and your Pisces stand a better chance seeking happiness elsewhere.

Thoughts...
He has his quirky sides which may charm you or annoy you - depending on your mood. Look beneath the surface.

THE FEMALE

YOUR DATE: PISCES
19 February–20 March

The Essence of her

Feminine – sweet, with an innocent attitude – lively, sparkling and socially active – tolerant and liberal – sensitive – slightly insecure – sensual and erotically assertive – kind, caring and understanding – extremely positive with a constructive outlook on life –a dreamer; easily inspired – creative – prone to escapism – an incurable romantic

...and remember: Flexibility and mutual understanding are very important. If she feels cornered, she will simply disappear into her dream world.

Blind Date – speedy essentials

Who's waiting for you?

She might be a little early, simply because she doesn't like being stressed before a date. You'll notice her right away... the smile, the sparkling laughter and the enthusiasm in her eyes. Although she may be talking to other men in the room as you arrive, she'll focus on you for the entire evening. Her femininity is not based on fancy clothes. She will keep it casual and comfortable. There's nothing snobbish about her. Luxurious brands are not important – if it looks good, it's fine.

Emergency fixes for embarrassing pauses.

A Pisces woman will make sure to keep the conversation going, especially if she suspects you are feeling nervous. Her conversation will be bubbly and casual. She won't delve into deep topics right away. She wants to get to know you and your personality. Should the conversation need a slight boost, talk about something unusual you've done or an exotic place you've visited.

Your place or mine?

Location doesn't matter, provided it's comfortable and convenient. She doesn't go on blind dates looking for casual sex –but if you've managed to capture her attention, she will be open to it. An invitation to 'continue the night somewhere else' should be casual, without direct implications of anything erotic. If she joins you, it's because she's noticed something special about you – and not just your toolbox.

Checklist, before you dash out to meet her:
Text her the night before
(hint: Let her know you're excited)
Have ideas about an activity
(hint: Make it special: skydiving, etc.)
Wear simple and masculine attire
(hint: No polkadots or fancy pants)
Be close-shaved or have a groomed beard
(hint: Be well kept)
Prepare a few wine and food suggestions
(hint: But don't be a showoff)

Tip: The Pisces woman is one of the biggest surprises of the zodiac. She may be sparkling, feminine and a little girlish, but she has a sixth sense when it comes to pleasing men – both inside and outside of the bedroom.

CHAPTER 1

PREPARE YOURSELF

Catch her eye, capture her attention
Top 10 attention grabbers

1. A warm smile and a cheerful laugh.
2. Be charming, polite and confident.
3. Introduce her to something unusual that you're knowledgeable about.
4. Present her with a challenge you need solved.
5. Let her know you're a wizard in the kitchen – even if you can only make pizza.
6. Suggest a sporty outdoor activity, preferably something a little unusual.
7. Show compassion; offer a helping hand to strangers.
8. Notice the beauty around you: a nice sunset, falling leaves, etc.
9. Show your sensual side by enjoying your food and drink slowly.
10. Take her dancing.

The HE. The man!

Her ideal man probably lives on different planet – in any case, it's a tall order to find him on this one. Her expectations are high and sometimes unrealistic. However, she keeps searching, and she falls in love frequently. She needs a strong man: someone who makes her feel safe and protected from the world. He must also be sensitive, generous and adventurous. Being an attentive lover goes without saying. 'Earth to Pisces … please come in. Repeating, Earth to Pisces!'

The Essence of him

Tough and masculine– sensitive and understanding – adventurous – enjoys physical pursuits, preferably outdoors, but also cherishes cosy evenings at home – supportive of his partner professionally and protective of her emotionally – provides her with intimacy, comfort and security – understanding and kind – has an excellent sense of humour – erotically confident and playful

Pisces arousal meter

From 0 to 100… In 30 minutes – or three hours. Either she's ready for an erotic encounter, or she's not. Remember, she is sensitive and easily influenced by moods and atmospheres.

Remember: Be true to yourself

It doesn't matter if she is the most stunning girl you've ever met – if you don't match, you don't match. You may be able to put on a show for a while to hold her attention, but what's the point? We can't please everybody. We all have different needs, dreams, tastes and preferences. There's no such thing as a one-size-fits-all lover. Be yourself, and be true to who you are – always!

Very important: Never take a Pisces woman for granted. Let her know you appreciate everything she does for you – including during your more sensual moments.

CHAPTER 2

THE FIRST DATE

Getting your foot in the door
The basics

Let's talk about it. Be open about your problems. She is one of the most caring signs in the zodiac and will always be willing to help you.

Be reliable. A Pisces woman needs to feel secure, and a guy who only shows up when he feels like it will make her miserable. Show her that you are reliable. Being able to trust a man is important to her.

Tough cookie. Don't be fooled by her seemingly innocent or helpless personality; this woman is capable of punching your teeth in – at least metaphorically – when provoked.

Competition. Make a move. If she receives attention from another interesting male, she may leave you out in the cold.

Full package. Although she prefers masculinity and strength, she also values and respects a man's sensitive and romantic side. What she's really looking for is the whole package.

Genuine admiration. Let her know how you feel about her. Admire her looks, her ambition, her commitment... the lot.

Whatever you do...

- **DON'T** be slow to accept her suggestions.

- **DON'T** leave all of the decisions to her. Don't be indecisive. •

DON'T give her any reason to doubt you.

- **DON'T** expect frequent sex without commitment.

- **DON'T** try to save her feelings by telling white lies.

Remember,

It's important for her to establish a emotional connection with her man.

- **DON'T** be lazy or physically inactive.

- **DON'T** tout blunt or populist views.

- **DON'T** give the impression of being a free spirit who has no

intention of settling down.

- **DON'T** brag about your romantic or erotic adventures.

- **DON'T** be cheap. Act generously, and pamper her.

before she can relax and feel comfortable in the relationship.

Signs you're in - or not

The Pisces woman may not be a romantic, but she's in love with love – or at least her perception of love. Although she comes across as sweet and innocent, she is a smart woman who applies her femininity naturally. When you're on a date, she listens, understands, shows interest and smiles while gently touching your hand... You think 'Wow' and put your arms around her. However, she seems to be this friendly with everybody. How do you make sure it's you she's interested in? Pay attention to the following:

Chances are she will...

- invite you to her home or somewhere similarly intimate
- organise activities with friends and include you
- compliment you for being a Man
- seem carried away by your attention
- respond to your texts – quickly!
- appreciate your physical attention: hugs, touches and gentle kisses

Not your type? Making an exit

This woman believes in love – and she believes in miracles, too. If she feels you may have a problem, she'll be right there by your side, helping you to resolve it. If she has a problem? There's always chocolate and a bottle of wine. If the relationship is struggling, she'll want to fix it. How difficult it is to leave her depends on how long you've been together, how well she knows you – and whether she really loves you. If she does, she'll have convinced herself that you have a few things that need sorting out. If these are a few things you don't want to sort out, it might be a good idea to stop the initiative before it starts. Remember, she is sensitive. It might be a very good idea to have a casual chat or two before getting blunt about it.

Foolproof exit measures:

To most people, these actions may seem like nothing more than a hassle – but to the female Pisces, it's serious stuff – and hurtful. Make sure you know what you want before you go ahead with it.

- Insist on being passive during sex
- When you open a gift from her, sigh and say, 'Oh well, it's the thought that counts'
- Criticise her family and friends
- Always choose the cheapest option, no matter what you're doing
- Keep in touch with female friends and ex-girlfriends
- Be indecisive about most things and never let her know where you stand

CHAPTER 3

SEX'N STUFF

Seductive moves:
How to get her in the mood:

If she's in the right frame of mind, it won't take much. Even the smallest hint about sex can funnel her thoughts toward it. It's not that she has a dirty mind – merely fine-tuned sensual antennas. The fact that she may even interpret innocent suggestions erotically just adds a bit of spice to her personality.

Preferences and erotic nature

A seductive look, a sensual touch, a kiss that lasts a moment longer than expected: subtle hints, which other women in the zodiac probably wouldn't even notice, make her shiver with anticipation. She's very receptive to visual stimulation, no matter how innocent. Watching a chick flick with a few erotic scenes is enough to make her hot – and slightly embarrassed, if you've only just met each other. She is easily turned on. However, a man who expects sex without the fun of seduction turns her off. She is sensitive to people taking her for granted, and this applies to an erotic partner as well – maybe even more so.

Hitting the right buttons

Although every sign has areas on the body that are more sensitive than others, individual sensitivity may vary quite a bit. Don't go body-blind. Honing in on these erogenous zones and forgetting the rest of her is not a good idea. Use these areas to create sparks while turning her on, and as a passion-booster when things get heated. Watch her body language – including the most obvious of signs. Open your mind to the sensuality of touch and taste.

Key areas
Her feet

Get it on
You will notice that her feet are pretty, regardless of whether she's wearing nail varnish or not. Pisces women seem to be blessed with beautiful feet that are soft, pleasant and smooth– and very sensitive to sensual attention.

Arouse her
Now, this is a little tricky. Men's feet seldom make the list of their most attractive features – at least not according to most women. That's why playing footsies can be risky. However, if you have well-kept feet to show off, go ahead and gently brush them over hers. Remember to pay attention to her feet during sex as well. Gentle kisses can produce serious sparks.

Surprise her

While watching TV, give her a nice foot massage with some lotion or oil. Whereas other women might fall asleep, the Pisces woman will wake up. Take your time, be gentle and allow her to get into it.

Spice it up

Let her use her feet to touch and caress you. Use plenty of oil and let her play. Be creative about it...

Remember: The Pisces woman enjoys a masculine partner in bed. Be sensitive to her needs, but don't ask how she feels every two minutes.

Her expectations

Making waves. If she could, the Pisces woman would prefer to make love on a waterbed. She finds the movements created by water to be stimulating, seductive and highly erotic.

Masculine vibes. Although her sex drive is strong and her passion intense, she doesn't enjoy taking command in bed. She usually feels more comfortable with a strong partner.

Close the window. If she's stimulated in the right way, she may turn out be a loud lover, inclined to thoroughly express her pleasure. It might be a good idea to close the window before you get started.

Close attention... One of her favourite ways of arousing her partner is to kiss and suck him all over. This demands an awful lot of patience – and she loves it.

Bring on the fantasies. Erotic daydreams are the spice of her sensual life, and she doesn't mind trying out a few fantasies. However, in order to fully enjoy the adventure, she needs a partner who's just as excited as she is.

Your sensual preferences
Quiz yourself and find out whether this woman is for you.

Where on the scale are you?
1 = Don't agree | 3 = Sure | 5 = Agree!

1. Intensity, passion and creativity make for a good erotic cocktail.
One a scale for 1 to 5, you are: 1 - 2 - 3- 4 - 5

2. Too much talk and reassurance can rob sex of some of its impulsiveness.
One a scale for 1 to 5, you are: 1 - 2 - 3- 4 - 5

3. A sensual erotic life is more important than frequent sex.
One a scale for 1 to 5, you are: 1 - 2 - 3- 4 - 5

4. Expressiveness is important during sex.
One a scale for 1 to 5, you are: 1 - 2 - 3- 4 - 5

Score.
15 - 20: Sex is not only frequent, but also sensual, passionate and highly erotic. Enjoy!
10 - 14: She may surprise you from time to time by transforming from a sweet and innocent girl to a sassy and confident babe. The variety will spice up your erotic life.
05 - 09: Never overlook her little hints. Don't take away the magic by asking questions – just gently play along. Her suggestions can make the days very sensual. Take time to enjoy and explore it.
01 - 04: Either she's too much for you, or you are too fixed in your ways. Maybe the two of you are simply misinterpreting each other. Try communicating more.

CHAPTER 4

GENERAL STUFF

The big picture

Keep in mind that the characteristics of a Pisces may vary quite a bit depending on where within the sign she was born, as well as a wide range of additional astrological factors. But for now, let's stick to the basics. Just remember: don't jump to conclusions as soon as you meet her. Give her room to shine. Get to know the woman behind the sign.

Her personality: Pros and cons

Pros	Cons
• Feminine and bubbly	• Naïve
• Romantic	• Seldom satisfied or fulfilled
• Sensitive	• Irrational
• Compassionate	• Changes partners – often
• Charming and social	• Dates the wrong men – often
• Understanding	• Emotional; a dreamer
• Passionate and sensual	• Tries to 'save' men
• Uniquely optimistic	• Easily hurt and offended
• Gets on with different people	• Prone to escapism
• Loyal and supportive	• Overindulgent; sex, food etc
• Energetic	• Overly flirty
• Has an appetite for life	• Conflict-averse
• Open-minded	• Too eager to please
• Affectionate	• Insecure

Tip: How to show romantic interest

Be a tad old-fashioned about it. Show your masculinity and woo her. Invite her out, offer to help her with a practical task, bring a small gift or a flower... Chivalry is a good approach. She will appreciate it.

Romantic Vibes

Miss Pisces:
The romantic and supportive partner

The essence

Dreamy. She is incredibly idealistic – not when it comes to love, but when it comes to men. When she finally finds someone who's on her level, she will be attentive, supportive and loyal.

Constructive compassion. She's fascinated by a guy with a story. Throw in a personal challenge, and she'll be captivated. Her amazingly positive attitude makes her believe she can turn him around and make him happy. Well, reality tends to kick in after a while, and she'll be off on her next adventure.

Security. Although she is perfectly capable of taking care of herself, she longs for a strong man to keep her safe. The Pisces woman tends to settle down with someone who can provide comfort and security – but even so, she craves romance.

A soulmate. She needs a man who sees the same colours as she does – in every aspect of life. She needs to feel alive – and to live!

Make it real. She's not just a dreamer; she actually pursues her romantic dreams, and she wants her man to join her.

Harmony. She will strive to make life comfortable in every way. A Pisces' home is a happy one.

Tip: How to show erotic interest

You don't have to work hard at this. She is very sensitive to erotic suggestions, or even suggestions that she may interpret as erotic. Give her something to wonder about, something that may be erotic ... or maybe not. Tease her a little.

Erotic Vibrations

Miss Pisces:
The warm and tender lover

The essence

Sassy intuition. The Pisces woman seems to have a sixth sense when it comes to doing the right things to get her partner in the mood for sex.

Fun and frisky. She is ultra-feminine, but also determined and passionate. Although she may strike you as soft and maybe even a little timid, she can be a wild thing in bed.

Creative input. Suggestions will be received with enthusiasm – provided they don't offend her sensitive nature.

Genuine. She is tolerant, liberal and patient – a brilliant combination! There's nothing pretentiously cool about her. She is genuinely enthusiastic and easily aroused. A quick look through a dirty magazine is usually all it takes to get her started.

Hot! ...or not! For her, there's no such thing as being mildly interested. Either she's turned on or she's not.

Considerate and tender. She will always strive to please her partner - and handle his tired body with patience. She's a dream come true for any man's ego.

CHAPTER 5

COMPATIBILITY QUIZ

Are you banging your head against the wall, or does she unleash your positive potential? Do you provoke her or bring out the best in her? Is she making you throw your arms into the air in exasperation, or do you feel inspired and complete in her company? Take the test to find out.

Question 1.
Do you regard flexibility as a strength?

A - Not necessarily. It can actually be a sign of weakness and insecurity.
B - Being flexible is very important. It allows you to get more out of life.
C - Flexibility can get you in touch with interesting people.

Question no 2
Do you think erotic fantasies make you a better lover?

A - Yes. Fantasies make you inherently more creative.
B - Nope! Daydreaming is nothing but a waste of time.
C - It may, provided the fantasies don't stay in your head.

(cont.)

Question no 3
What does sex mean to you?

A – Playfulness, romance and loads of fun.
B – Tenderness, affection and sensuality.
C – Pure physical pleasure.

Question no 4
Does it bother you when a woman is very sensitive and easily hurt?

A - Yes. I find it difficult to speak my mind with someone who might take things too personally.
B – Not really. I try not to step on anybody's toes anyway.
C - Not at all. I respect and love sensitive girls.

Question no 5
Do you enjoy an energetic partner, generally speaking?

A - Absolutely. Life is an adventure. Why waste it?
B – Not really. Women who need to be doing something all the time wear me out.
C - Yes, provided we can do things together.

Question no 6
You find yourself in bed with a woman who you initially thought was sweet and cuddly. How do you react when she turns out to be a red-hot lover?

A – I'm not into surprises – especially not in bed. It would put me off.
B - What more could a man ask for? I'd love it!
C – I'd be a little shocked, but I'm sure I'd enjoy it – and her!

Question no 7
Do you enjoy dating a woman who treats you like you're the only man in the world?

A - That depends on how much I like her. I don't want to feel cornered.
B - I don't like that. Freedom and independence are important – for both of us.
C - Of course. Who wouldn't want to be pampered with attention?

Question no 8
Do you find it easy to kiss and make up after a fight?

A – Unfortunately, no. I'm too proud.
B - No problem. What's the point of being angry for days?
C - Yes, but only if the forgiveness is mutual.

Question no 9
Do you tend to rush your partner when you're aroused?

A - Never. I believe in allowing things to develop at their own pace.
B - Sometimes, but only if I'm really hot.
C - Yes. What's the point of dragging things out when you're ready?

Question no 10
Is it important to you that a woman knows exactly what how to arouse and satisfy you?

A – Yes, of course. What's the point of having sex if she doesn't please me?
B - Not right away. Everybody needs a bit of time to get to know their partner's needs.
C - Although it would be nice, I can't expect my partner to be a mind-reader.

SCORE	A	B	C
Question 1	1	10	5
Question 2	10	1	5
Question 3	5	10	1
Question 4	1	5	10
Question 5	10	1	5
Question 6	1	10	5
Question 7	5	1	10
Question 8	1	10	5
Question 9	1	5	10
Question 10	10	1	5

75 − 100

All of a sudden the days are crackling with energy. Life feels comfortable and exciting – including your erotic life. The two of you know that sensuality is important. Since you share the same needs and values, you don't have to work too hard to achieve them. Sex will never be boring between you. You'll try a lot of different things, but never anything that could upset either of you. Keep going as you are, and this will grow into a happy, positive, caring and sensual relationship.

51 − 74

If you're not at home gazing into each other's eyes, you're probably out and about together, getting to know new people and visiting exciting places. Not only is your life going to be filled with exciting sex, it will be romantic, too. You'll never allow grey days or details ruin this wonderful relationship. Never mind silly arguments and stupid upsets; just let it slide and move on. Life is short, and the adventures to come are many. You both realise that in order to live life to the fullest, you'll need to communicate and be on the same level. Full steam ahead!

26 – 50

Well, this relationship has a bit of everything. Plenty of joy and excitement, but also moments of doubt and frustration. There's wonderful sex, but also times when you could do without the hassle. In short, you're facing a roller coaster of emotions, adventures, expectations – and disappointments. It can work. It can be great. Or it could be a pain – something that holds you both back. The keys to success are communication, understanding and mutual goals. If even talking about it is too much trouble, why delay the exit? If you don't do something, you'll both be completely drained before long.

10 – 25

Soft and sensitive. Cute, feminine and cuddly. Not really your thing, huh? She has many sides to her personality: she can be tough, firm and straight to the point – at least in her professional life. Her private and romantic life? Well, that's a different story. She is a flower, a poet and a delicate woman who needs careful attention. She wants a man to be a man. If you're not prepared to take on that responsibility, or if you want a strong woman who can boss you around a bit, you'll have to look somewhere else. Sure, you can try to talk it over, but at some point, you'll have to make up your mind.

Thoughts...
Her moods may confuse you a little
at times - or maybe you are being
insensitive to her needs without
knowing.

Love rules. Embrace it.

...just a final note:
This book has not been approved by your date and should be treated accordingly. He or she *may* not agree with the content.

www.ingramcontent.com/pod-product-compliance
Lightning Source LLC
Chambersburg PA
CBHW071838020426
42331CB00007B/1781